ADJOA'S
Paddling Pool

WRITTEN BY
IZZIE KPOBIE-MENSAH

ILLUSTRATED BY
LEANNE ARMSTRONG

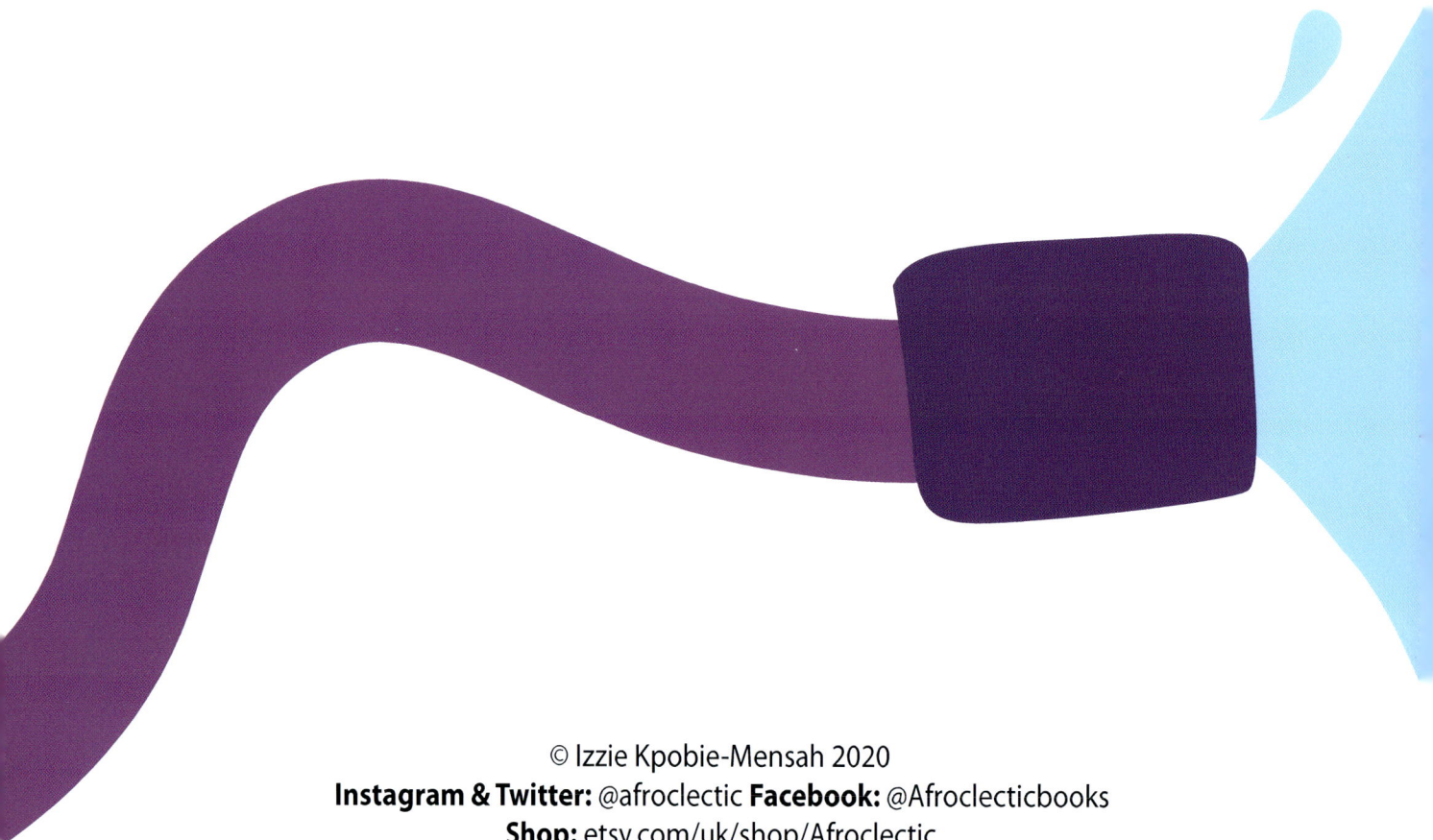

Instagram & Twitter: @afroclectic **Facebook:** @Afroclecticbooks
Shop: etsy.com/uk/shop/Afroclectic

Illustrator, Leanne Armstrong
Instagram: @leanne_creative **Email:** leanne@leannecreative.com

Other books by Izzie Kpobie-Mensah:
Adjoa Goes To Nursery

2

This book belongs to

....

To Mum

Thank you, Miss you, Love You.

For my children and grandchildren

Adjoa, Serwaa, Kwesi, Akua and Enrica and Gabriella who always inspire me.

For Kennedy
Who encourages me to be the best I can be.

For My Family
Who support my creativity warts and all.

Remembering those who were part of my journey and now of blessed memory. Loving you always xx

Adjoa is a very lively 3-year-old who lives in a ground floor flat in South London, with a garden where she likes to have an adventure every day.

It was a hot summer's day
and mummy was tidying the house.

Adjoa decided that she wanted to play outside in her garden.

In the garden, there was a medium sized blue tub that mummy filled with water to make a paddling pool.

Adjoa decided that she wanted to paddle and asked mummy if she could put on her swimming costume and brand new trainers.

Adjoa changed into her swimming costume and brand new trainers. She also took some of her toys out into the garden with her...

A doll...

a ball...

and her bath toys!

Adjoa's mummy told her not to climb in the tub because she didn't want her to get her brand new trainers wet.

Adjoa was happy playing with her toys but really wanted to get into the tub and splash around.

When mummy turned around to mop the kitchen floor, Adjoa climbed into the tub.

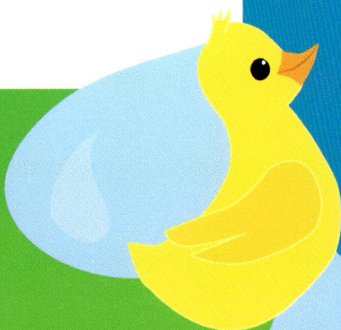

Adjoa had forgotten mummy's warning about her brand new trainers and started to play in the tub.

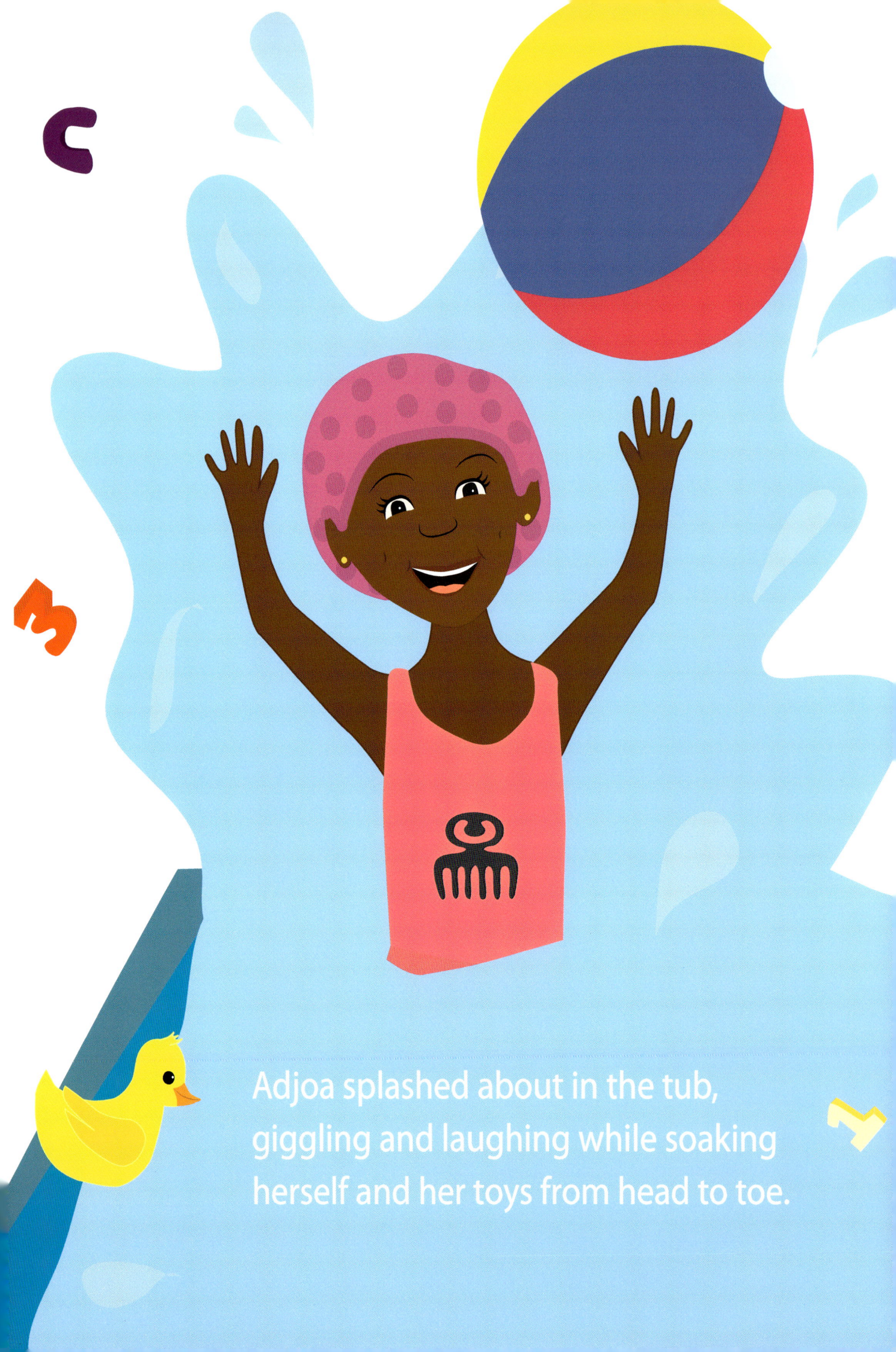

Adjoa splashed about in the tub, giggling and laughing while soaking herself and her toys from head to toe.

Mummy turned around
and saw Adjoa in the tub.

She was very cross and told Adjoa she was naughty for not listening.

Adjoa was very sorry
and promised not to
wear her brand new
trainers in the tub again.

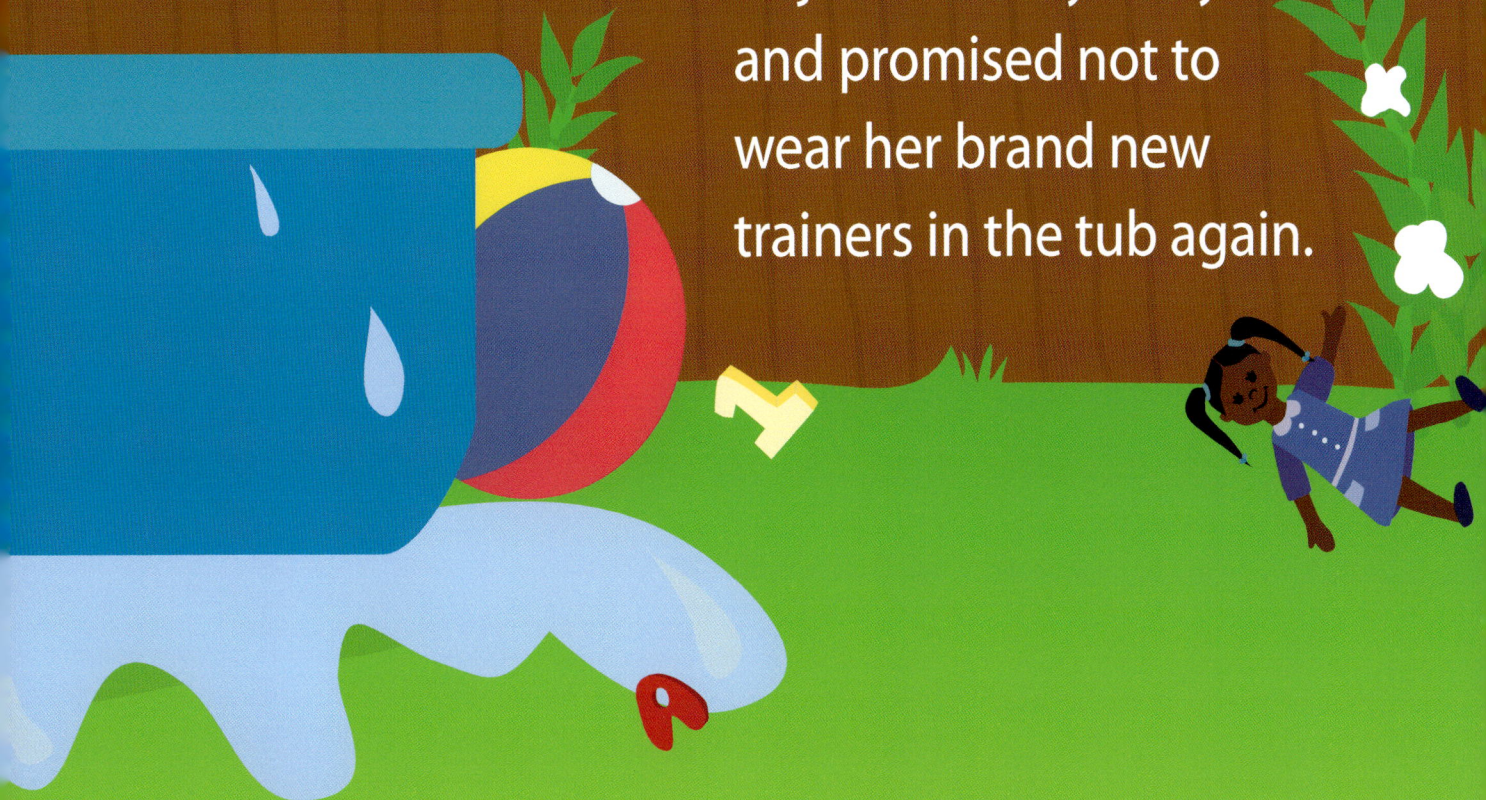

Luckily it was a hot day. So, Mummy hung the brand new trainers on the washing line.

The brand new trainers dried without any damage, ready for Adjoa to wear again.

Later in the evening,
Adjoa had a bath.

She splashed about
making bubbles.

Adjoa had such
a good time that
when she had finished
bathing, she rushed to
put on her pyjamas.

Adjoa fell asleep
on her daddy's lap
dreaming about the
adventure she would
have the next day.

Game!

What's your Ghanaian Day name?

Choose the day of the week you were born and find out!

Day of the week	Girl's name	Boy's name
Sunday	Akosua	Akwasi/Kwesi
Monday	Adjoa/Adwoa	Kojo/Kwadwo
Tuesday	Abena	Kwabena
Wednesday	Akua	Kwaku
Thursday	Yaa	Yaw
Friday	Afia	Kofi
Saturday	Amma	Kwame

Now you can use your own Ghanaian day name as the main character when you read this book again!

Adinkra Symbols

Adinkra Symbols used throughout this book represent brief sayings or phrases that express an opinion or make a statement of wisdom. They can be classed as original Akan Emoji's. The symbols are often handed down by tradition from generation to generation and in more recent times can be found on clothing, jewellery, furniture and many other items.

Symbol	Symbol name	Meaning
	Sankofa	Return and Get it (learning from the past)
	Duafe	Beauty
	Nyame Dua	Tree of God (protection)
	Akoma Ntoso	Understanding
	Nkyinkyim	Versatility
	Kwatakye Atiko	Bravery and Valour
	Akoma	The Heart
	Pempamsie	Readiness, Steadfastness, Hardiness
	Mpuannum	Loyalty

About the Author

Izzie Kpobie-Mensah has over 25 years of working in the National Health Service (NHS) and health care related organisations. Currently Izzie works on Equality, Diversity and Inclusion in Higher Education and through her external networks.

Inspired by the birth of her first grandchild, Izzie revisited the books she wrote for her children when they were younger and with the illustrative support from Leanne Armstrong the *Adventures of Adjoa Fordjour* have been brought to life.

This busy daughter, wife, mother, sister, aunt and grandma is an all-round crafter who also sews and makes beaded jewellery. When Izzie finds spare time, she can be found at craft fairs and family events with her bead buffet encouraging jewellery making for any age and any ability.

Her Motto: Inspiration is everywhere!

@afroclectic

@afroclecticbooks

Isabella 'Izzie' Kpobie-Mensah

etsy.com/shop/Afroclectic

Afroclectic.co.uk